Facts About the Binturong

By Lisa Strattin

© 2019 Lisa Strattin

FREE BOOK

FREE FOR ALL SUBSCRIBERS

LisaStrattin.com/Subscribe-Here

BOX SET

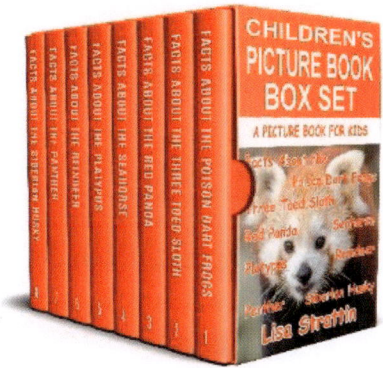

- FACTS ABOUT THE POISON DART FROGS
- FACTS ABOUT THE THREE TOED SLOTH
- FACTS ABOUT THE RED PANDA
- FACTS ABOUT THE SEAHORSE
- FACTS ABOUT THE PLATYPUS
- FACTS ABOUT THE REINDEER
- FACTS ABOUT THE PANTHER
- FACTS ABOUT THE SIBERIAN HUSKY

LisaStrattin.com/BookBundle

Facts for Kids Picture Books by Lisa Strattin

Little Blue Penguin, Vol 92

Chipmunk, Vol 5

Frilled Lizard, Vol 39

Blue and Gold Macaw, Vol 13

Poison Dart Frogs, Vol 50

Blue Tarantula, Vol 115

African Elephants, Vol 8

Amur Leopard, Vol 89

Sabre Tooth Tiger, Vol 167

Baboon, Vol 174

Sign Up for New Release Emails Here

LisaStrattin.com/subscribe-here

All rights reserved. No part of this book may be reproduced by any means whatsoever without the written permission from the author, except brief portions quoted for purpose of review.

All information in this book has been carefully researched and checked for factual accuracy. However, the author and publisher makes no warranty, express or implied, that the information contained herein is appropriate for every individual, situation or purpose and assume no responsibility for errors or omissions. The reader assumes the risk and full responsibility for all actions, and the author will not be held responsible for any loss or damage, whether consequential, incidental, special or otherwise, that may result from the information presented in this book.

All images are free for use or purchased from stock photo sites or royalty free for commercial use.

Some coloring pages might be of the general species due to lack of available images.

I have relied on my own observations as well as many different sources for this book and I have done my best to check facts and give credit where it is due. In the event that any material is used without proper permission, please contact me so that the oversight can be corrected.

COVER IMAGE

https://www.flickr.com/photos/sheilaellen/1122131130/

ADDITIONAL IMAGES

https://www.flickr.com/photos/15016964@N02/6605860661/

https://www.flickr.com/photos/joejungmann/13917661466/

https://www.flickr.com/photos/anneliekeb/9092132081/

https://www.flickr.com/photos/28450828@N02/48391086492/

https://www.flickr.com/photos/28450828@N02/48391086002/

https://www.flickr.com/photos/19598613@N00/762624878

https://www.flickr.com/photos/andyhay/43389969075/

https://www.flickr.com/photos/118566686@N08/21816145533/

https://www.flickr.com/photos/of_guido/7353426018/

https://www.flickr.com/photos/tammylo/8027519374/

Contents

INTRODUCTION 9

BEHAVIOR 11

APPEARANCE 13

REPRODUCTION 15

LIFE SPAN 17

SIZE 19

HABITAT 21

DIET 23

ENEMIES 25

SUITABILITY AS PETS 27

INTRODUCTION

The Binturong is an animal that lives in the Southeast Asia forests. They are related to Fossas and Mongooses, having the same kind of long snout.

BEHAVIOR

The Binturong likes to be alone and mostly comes out at night in the trees. They cannot leap from tree to tree, so have to climb down to the ground and then back up another tree. They are very good climbers, using their claws and strong tails to help in hanging on to branches and the tree trunk as they move around. They also are good swimmers, so they jump into the water to cool off from the sun's heat when they are out during the daytime.

APPEARANCE

The Binturong has long, shaggy fur that can be dark brown or black, with gray tips at the ends. They also have long hairs at the top of their ears. They have white whiskers, like a cat, that are sensitive and thick, on their cheeks and above their eyes!

REPRODUCTION

Most Binturongs mate during February and April or July and November, although they have been known to mate all year round. The female is pregnant for only 3 months, then she has her cubs in a nest she has made on the ground, surrounded by vegetation. This is to keep her babies safe from weather and predators as much as possible. The babies nurse from their mother for about 2 months and stay with her for the first year or so. Then they are grown to their adult size and can live on their own.

LIFE SPAN

The Binturongs live for 10 to 15 years in the wild, but have been known to live as long as 25 years in zoos or habitat captivity.

SIZE

The Binturong grows to be 2 to 3 feet long and weighs between 20 and 30 pounds, on average.

HABITAT

The Binturong lives in thick, dense forests where they can find plenty of protective cover in the trees and on the ground to stay clear of any predators. They prefer the areas where there are few people, so when people move into their native range, the Binturongs move further away. They used to be found in great numbers in Thailand, China, Cambodia, India, Malaysia, Laos, the Philippines, the island of Borneo and Laos. But there are not as many in the wild as they used to be. This is mainly because of the decline of the native jungles where they live.

DIET

The Binturong is classified as a carnivore, meaning they eat meat. But they mostly eat fruit! They will sometimes eat insects, rodents and birds, but they really prefer fruit. They are able to climb trees like a cat and use their feet and claws to dig and rip open the fruit they find. In the water, they even catch fish. So they do eat animals and fruit. Knowing this about them, it is a bit surprising that they are not classed as an omnivore.

ENEMIES

Even though the Binturong is a slow animal, they are not really prey to many animals in the wild. They do have to watch out for large Birds of Prey, Tigers and Snakes though. These animals like to catch and kill the Binturong.

SUITABILITY AS PETS

The Binturong has been kept as a pet in some areas, but you would probably need a special exotic pet license. You should check your local laws if you want to keep one, that is, if you could find a place to buy one at all.

It is probably a better idea for you to visit a zoo where they have a suitable habitat for them and watch the Binturong there.

COLOR ME

COLOR ME

COLOR ME

COLOR ME

COLOR ME

COLOR ME

COLOR ME

COLOR ME

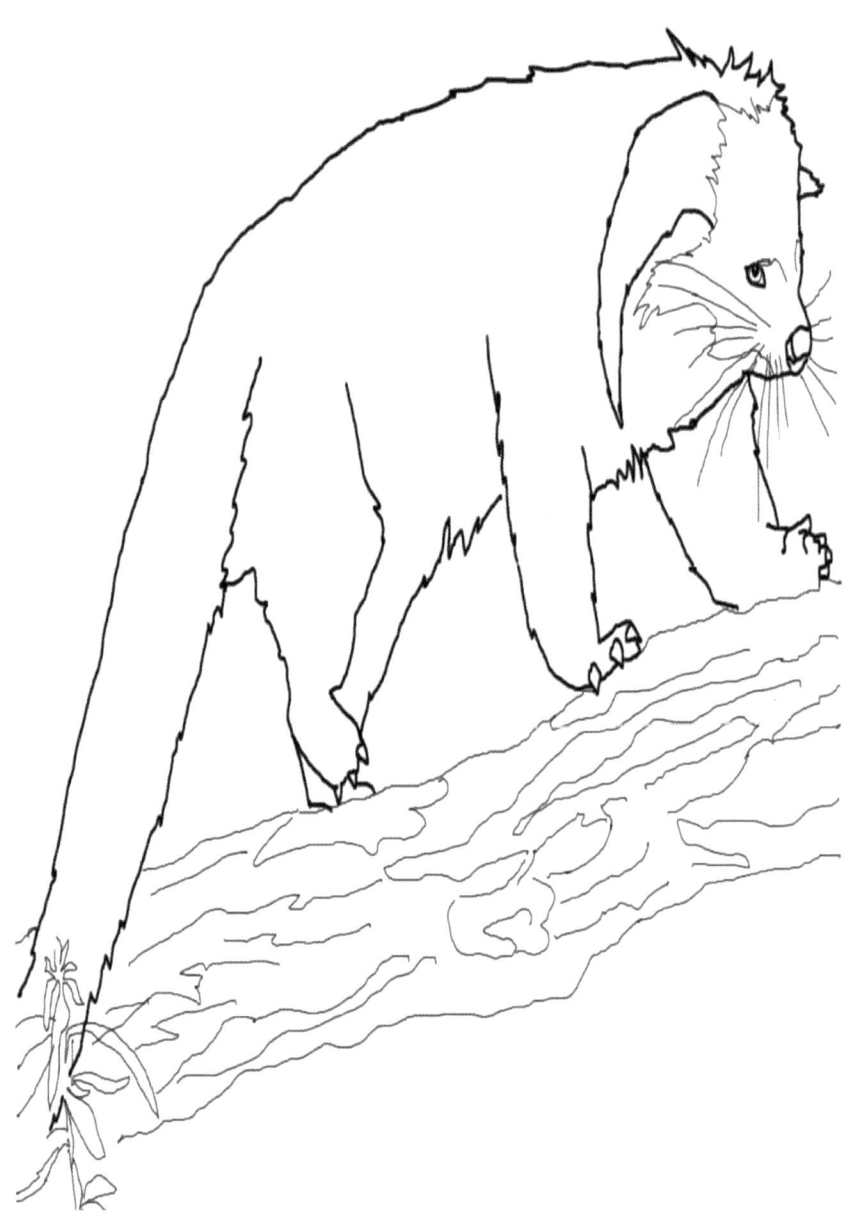

COLOR ME

37

COLOR ME

Please leave me a review here:

LisaStrattin.com/Review-Vol-335

For more Kindle Downloads Visit Lisa Strattin Author Page on Amazon Author Central

amazon.com/author/lisastrattin

To see upcoming titles, visit my website at LisaStrattin.com– most books available on Kindle!

LisaStrattin.com

FREE BOOK

FOR ALL SUBSCRIBERS – SIGN UP NOW

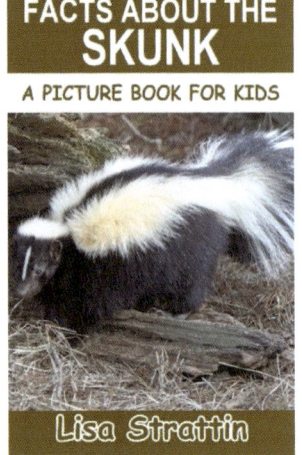

LisaStrattin.com/Subscribe-Here

LisaStrattin.com/Facebook

LisaStrattin.com/Youtube

Printed in Great Britain
by Amazon